The Art of Reading People

How to Avoid (or End) an Abusive Relationship by Dealing with Toxic People and Manipulation (2022 Guide for Beginners)

Harmony Davison

Contents

INTRODUCTION

The ability to correctly assess and analyses people is a valuable skill that can assist you in navigating life and making sensible judgments. This is a talent that some people are endowed with. Spend some time with them in a room, and they can read you from cover to cover like a book. If you lack the talent, you should not be concerned. You may learn it as well. For example, no one is born into the FBI. Recruits are trained and taught how to read individuals. You, too, can learn.

You may not utilize your expertise to prevent the following terrorist incident, but you can use it to avoid subtle acts of personal terrorism in your life.

Today's world is confusing. Simple days and life is gone now; people were content to live simple, humdrum lives. Today, there is a race going on everywhere, and everyone is attempting to be the best at something. Most of the time, this occurs at the expense of someone else.

How well do you know the people in your life? What role do you have in their lives, and what role do they play in yours? What role do you play in your social circle? People analysis entails more than just seeing them and their body language. It all comes down to awareness. When you become aware of another person's point of view, you gain a new perspective on life. This level of understanding necessitates that you transcend yourself, leave your mood, and embrace theirs before deciding for them. Awareness brings you closer to individuals since it allows you to comprehend their life views, habits, attitudes, worries, thoughts, dislikes, rules, values, and preferences. You see them for who they are rather than what you believe they are. You see someone without the psychological deceit that passes through your mind, and you completely accept them. That is how you make meaningful connections with others. You may learn to read someone by paying attention to the crucial things they do – which are usually involuntary behaviours – and you can learn a lot about them. You can show a side of them that the rest of the world is unaware of. You may not be a psychic or have the ability to read people's minds or foresee the future, but you may observe and be astonished by what you learn about them.

CHAPTER 1

HOW TO READ PEOPLE

How do you read a person like a book? People are like books, and just like the agonizing process of identifying facts and data in a book, you must spend a significant amount of time analyzing people's motives and feelings before forming definitive conclusions about the types ofpersonalities such people 'carry' within themselves. As a result, personalities are also known as carriage, attitude, behaviour, position, and posture.

Personality analysis is a mysterious concept with certain vital secrets that you can grasp to have strong hints about who a person is. Understanding the traits of an individual, whether they are a crush or a professional colleague, is crucial for better and faster comprehension.

You can read individuals like a book by observing and judging their behaviour, body language, and attire in that order.

Reading People Based on Their Behavior

Everyone expresses deep-seated and intrinsic ideas and feelings through their actions through conduct. You can't give something you don't have, even though many people try to be someone they're not. Because the truth can never be held for long, it tends to win over time. Most of the time, a simple smile or chuckle can reveal someone's true nature and conduct. You'd be able to tell if someone is faking a grin if, for example, your partner's eyes aren't blinking when they are smiling with reversed lips. You may be distrustful of their actions.

You can read about changes in someone's behaviour by looking at the posture of their arms when they're talking to you, such as how they fold their arms and cross their legs when they're talking to you. Additionally, the position of the hands and legs can reveal emotional traumas and psychological changes in a person.

Have you ever met someone who used words to try to dominate and affect you? That is an indication of someone who craves power. If you can carefully monitor and interpret someone's behavioural tendencies and attitudes over time, you can predict their future actions and understand the motivations behind their actions and decisions.

Another technique to read and decode a person's behaviour is to observe how they interact with others. Do they always make an effort to restore shattered bridges between people? Are they gregarious and friendly? When a person exhibits these characteristics, it is safe to assume that they are kind and cheerful.

It is great to read someone to comprehend the quality and level of their personality. This will help you understand what motivates people to create attainable goals. They are prouder of their accomplishments than their teamwork most of the time.

Reading People Using Body Language

Body language is one method for reading and analyzing someone's attitudes and behaviours. The movement of a person's eyes can reveal the truth of what they are saying. If the individual avoids eye contact with your own eyes, scurries his gaze on you, and stares at you for an extended period, he may be lying. Also, if your spouse isn't performing all of these things, he might be lying.

Whether a person is constantly checking messages on his phone and looking at his wristwatch, you may read and notice when they are not serious about your interactions—paying close attention to their employees rather than you is another clue that they are uninterested in your chats. These actions may also imply that they are bored with your discourse and are looking for ways to keep you away.

Allowing your intuition to register and decode a person's silent and subconscious expressions is one of the most effective methods to read that person like a book. It may appear in a flash of light at times, but if you do not pick it up right away, you may miss it later. How often does your crush or boyfriend blink their eyes during a meeting? Constant blinking indicates nervousness and unease.

 Although, in most circumstances, it is one of a person's traits of attractiveness and seduction. According to human psychological analysis, it is a symptom of anxiety, dread, and a more significant effect for persuasion. Reading someone's body language is like reading a book. As a result, a glance at someone might reveal a lot about them. Pursing the lips, for example, indicates fear, anxiety, or surprise, but clinched jaws indicate physical strain and tensions.

When your partner feels anxious and strained, they will rub their fingers on the back of the neck and lean away from you. Without equivocation, you should recognize that he is generally tired and irritated when someone begins to exhibit these characteristics.

Reading People Based on Their Appearance or Clothing

'Looks is deceiving,' as the saying goes, but reading people like a book cannot be overstated as another way of establishing whom a person is or telling about the work or profession that individual is engaged in through their appearance through the types of clothing they wear. For example, if someone wears a suit, you can assume they are a lawyer or banker; if they wear a lab coat, they are a scientist; if they wear a uniform, they are a military officer or police officer; and overalls splashed with paint indicate they are a painter.

The creases and wrinkles on a person's face can also reveal their age. Looking at the beginning, neck, and eyes, you will notice some lines or wrinkles, indicating that you are not too youthful.

If a person appears in faded clothes, you may deduce that they are not very wealthy; yet, they appear in high-quality clothes, designer shoes, purses, wristwatches, or even having a tidy haircut or hairdo can indicate a display of riches or a desire to be wealthy.

Furthermore, the individual's appearance and clothing can reveal whether or not he is a picky person. Is the individual dressed neatly, has a nice haircut, and is more concerned with their first impression? Some people may prefer to be worried and detail-oriented about their professions rather than their physical appearances.

Reading a person like a book will assist you to know when to engage in small talk with them. Starting conversations in this manner will encourage individuals to open up and talk with you.

CHAPTER 2

FACIAL SIGNALS

One of the crucial ways to portray emotions and moods is through facial expressions and the eyes. We can better comprehend what others are saying to us by learning and observing facial expressionsthat move faces rather than static objects.

We also form opinions about people's personalities and other characteristics based on what we perceive in their looks. People with appealing features, for example, are frequently assigned traits that they may or may not possess.

Although not all messages sent by facial expressions are susceptible to being consciously recognized by the interlocutor, it is generally known that the imperceptible movement of others' spoken communication affects our impressions of them.

First Impressions and the Face

The initial five minutes of the first meeting between two people are usually the most significant. The impressions produced in such a brief period are likely to last. This can even be reinforced by later action, which is frequently evaluated subjectively rather than objectively based on those initial impressions.

Because the face is one of the first things we notice about someone, it can play an essential role in forming relationships with people.

Sometimes, we form opinions about your character, personality, intelligence, temperament, ability to work, personal routines, and even your comfort as a friend or lover.

Face-to-Face Communication

Together with the eyes, the face is the most effective nonverbal communication tool. We use it to communicate how delighted we are as people, to reflect our current state of mind, to show the attention we devote to others, and so on, and the judgments of others are based on the clues they receive. On the other hand, facial expressions can be utilized to reinforce the impact of spoken signals, such as when a mother scolds her child, the look on her face indicates how upset she is.

Although other areas of the body contribute to how we utilize body language, we should not presume that a message is clear and entirely delivered by a single part of the body.

Although the range of expressions is vast, there are just a few emotions that most of us can reliably identify. Paul Ekman and Wallace Friesen discovered six distinct facial expressions:

Smiles

Light, standard, and huge smiles are all possible. They are typically employed as a greeting gesture to communicate various degrees of pleasure, enthusiasm, and happiness. When they like something, even blind youngsters smile. Their beauty and cheerfulness distinguish them. Smiles can sometimes be used to conceal other feelings:

- Maintain a cheerful demeanour in order to hide your difficulties.
- As a submission answer, smile.
- Smiling makes stressful situations less stressful.
- Smiling to draw other people's smiles.
- Smiling relieves tension.
- Smile to hide your fear.
-

Disappointment, Sadness, and Depression

They are identified by a lack of expression and traits such as a downward tilt of the corners of the lips, a low glance, and general architectural deterioration. Usually, these emotions are accompanied by a reduced voice level or a slower speech rate.

Although they are difficult to identify in most circumstances, other physical aspects ensure that we know which emotion is being expressed as:

Sadness

- Eyebrows form a semi arch when they are slightly inclined towards the ears.
- Shoulders regularly deteriorated.
- The commissures are inclining at 45 per cent of their typical range.
- Place your hands together and face down.
- Disappointment The brows are not adequately arched.
- Turning around and looking down, usually to the left.
- Shoulders slightly down, hands at the sides of the body

Depression

- Normally slanted brows
- A modest lowering tilt of the commissures.
- Shoulders lowered.
- Keep your legs and thighs parallel to each other.

However, we must keep in mind that each feeling is unique to the individual. Not everyone exhibits the same factions.

Dislike or disdain

They show their feelings by shrinking their eyes and puckering their lips. To avoid having to stare at the source of such a reaction, the nose is frequently wrinkled, and the head is tilted sideways. It is the only facial expression in only one area of the face, namely the centre. One end of the upper lip is elevated while the opposing side remains in place.

Anger

Fury is generally characterized by staring into the source of the insult, clenched teeth, and closed mouth, and eyes and brows slightly inclined to express anger. Safe hands pressing and containing the emotion can also be seen in an angry situation.

Fear

Fear is not a singular mode of expression that displays its presence. It might be seen as wide eyes, an open mouth, or a general tremor that affects the face and the rest of the body.

Interest

It is frequently diagnosed by what is known as a "bird's head," in which the head tilts at an angle towards the object of attention. Other characteristics include wider-open eyes and a somewhat open mouth. Another factor to consider is how complements are used in nonverbal messages. Because compliments alter our look, we must evaluate how they affect others' perceptions of us. This implies that we do not consistently deliver the nonverbal messages we wish to send. The more we are conscious of the difficulties of using body language without words, the better we will be able to use it.

Other Facts About the Face

Facial expressions are used to reflect the personality, attitudes toward people, sexual attraction and attractiveness, the desire to speak or begin a connection, and the degree of expressiveness during communication, in addition to emotions. Women laugh and smile more frequently than men, which may or may not be attributable to increased sociability or delight. They may be uncomfortable with the circumstance. During the dialogue, the expression on the face changes constantly. Among the modifications are the so-called "micro-momentary" facial expressions. This time is a fraction of a second, as the name implies, and it frequently reveals a person's actual feelings.

Laughter

Laughter is a physiological response produced by the body to particular stimuli. A grin is seen as a soft and silent kind of laughter. There are numerous views on its nature at the moment. The most recent high-impact studies have been conducted since 1999 by Robert Provine, a University of Maryland neurobiologist of behaviour, who stated that laughter is a "babbling playful, instinctive, contagious, stereotyped, and control unconscious, or involuntary – which rarely occurs in solitude." Laughter in humans begins at four months of life on average. According to current scientific studies, it is a sort of intrinsic communication acquired from monkeys and closely related to language.

For other scholars, such as Charles R. Gruner of the University of Georgia (1978), laughing is reminiscent or synonymous with the fighter's triumphant shout after defeating his opponent. Ensures an aggressive gesture in all forms of humour, even in the most harmless circumstances. According to Gruner, "even an infant laugh, not out of gratitude, but because he got what he wanted." According to philosopher John Morreall (1983), the biological origin of human laughter may be in a shared expression of relief after passing through the danger – the laxity we feel after laughing can help inhibit the aggressive response, turning laughter into a sign of behaviour that indicates trust in classmates.

In any event, the current study on orangutans and chimps suggests that they can laugh, implying that laughter has an evolutionary and genetic foundation.

It is commonly regarded as an external expression of amusement, associated with joy and happiness, in response to humorous moments or situations. Even though, according to various studies, such as those conducted by Robert Provine, laughter is driven by a funny stimulus in a minority of ordinary cases. It frequently appears as a more or less faked emotional complement to spoken communication and in stressful situations or amusing acts like tickling. According to specific medical ideas, laughter positively impacts health and well-being because it releases endorphins.

Various Types of Laughter

Laughter can vary in duration, tone, and features depending on the force with which it happens. As a result, we employ several words to characterize distinct forms of laughter, such as click, laugh, giggle, disdainful, frantic, uneasy, and equivocal laughter. Coquina, jingle, evil laugh, and hypoid are some of the other varieties.

Grin is the most contagious of all emotional cues because it promotes happy moods. The grin, like the laugh, is natural; even deaf and blind children smile. It usually appears at six weeks of age and is the human being's first language. It begins as physical activity and progresses to an emotional one. Smiling can be self-induced, which can improve our mood. Another virtue is that it stimulates the function of NK cells, which enhances our immune condition.

According to several research, laughter differs by gender: women laugh more singingly, while males laugh more snortingly or growlingly.

Laughter Physiology

It happens when an internal or external input is processed in the central nervous system's primary, secondary, and multimodal association areas. Emotions are processed in the limbic system, which is likely responsible for the potential motors that characterize laughing, such as facial expression and muscle movements that control breathing and phonation. Following the processing of the stimulus, in addition to the aforementioned automatic motor actions, a generalized autonomous activation is carried out, with an exit via numerous routes, including the hypothalamus-pituitary axis and the autonomic nervous system. All of these elements combine to form the feeling, a process that includes the motor act known as laughter in the case of joy.

The amygdala and the hippocampus are two limbic system structures implicated in creating laughter.

Several Investigations

Stimulating the subthalamic nucleus can cause laughter. It has been demonstrated in Parkinson's disease patients. Recent research by Itzhak Fried et al. from the University of California has allowed us to pinpoint a brain area known as the supplementary motor area, which, when stimulated with electrodes, causes a smile and, with more extreme stimulation, a loud laugh. The additional motor area is located near the language area. This mechanism was unintentionally found while treating a young woman with epilepsy.

Experiments have been carried out to determine where the sense of humour is located. In a study published in 2000 by scientists at the University of Rochester, volunteers were subjected to functional magnetic resonance imaging while being asked a series of questions. They concluded that this trait was concentrated in a limited frontal lobe portion. When a joke's grace resided in a pun, another London team ran the same test on participants who were told jokes. The results showed that the active brain area was the ventral prefrontal cortex, along with other regions involved in the linguistic process.

Medical Point of View

We laugh less and less each day. Children aged 7 to 10 laugh approximately 300 times per day, but adults who still laugh do so less than 80 times each day. Some people rarely laugh, and others do not feel the need to laugh at all.

Since the 1980s, studies by Psiconeuroinmunólogo Lee S. Berk and colleagues have established the sound effects of laughter:

• Some stress-related markers were reduced during laughter bouts, which was associated with lower adrenaline and cortisol levels.
• Laughter increases antibody production and the activation of defensive cells such as lymphocytes or cytotoxic T lymphocytes, which promote cellular immunity, which is vital in preventing tumour growth.
• The cheerful and repetitive laughter increased mood, lowered blood cholesterol levels, and regulated blood pressure.

Berk established a link between laughing and appetite more recently, in 2010. Laughter has been shown to increase hunger in the same way that moderate physical exercise does. According to this research, there is a simultaneous decrease in leptin levels and an increase in ghrelin levels in the blood.

Laughter has the following additional health benefits:

• Liberated from dread and sorrow.
• It aids in the reduction of rage.

•   It contributes to a shift in mental attitude that encourages disease reduction.

•   It helps digestion by increasing abdominal muscle contractions.

•   It helps with evacuation because of the "message" it gives the viscera.

•   It raises the heart rate and pulse, allowing "endorphin" hormones to perform one of their key jobs, such as preserving the flexibility of the coronary arteries.

•   Because it is an aerobic activity, it reduces the presence of cholesterol in the blood.

•   It aids in the reduction of blood glucose levels.

CHAPTER 3

HANDS

The hands have twenty-seven bones each and are an expressive feature of our bodies. They provide us with enormous capabilities as an advanced species in how we interact with our surroundings. The hands, after the face, are possibly the best source of body language.

It should be emphasized that hand gestures vary significantly among cultures, and what you consider a typical hand signal in one country may get you imprisoned in another.

A minor hand gesture could be used to reveal your subconscious thoughts. It can also be done with both hands while attempting to emphasize a point.

Important Hand Cues

Some of the essential hand indications in body language are as follows:

Holding

- Cupped hands form a container that can delicately hold something. Gripped hands can clutch something firmly. Hands can be carried together or separately. Cupped hands might represent a frail notion. They can also be used to give.
- Holding oneself can be an act of restriction as well. It could be to allow the other person to talk. It can also be used when a person is insane to keep them from acting violently.
- The tension in a holding group reflects the amount of pressure that an individual is under. Arms that are folded can be released. However, it gets more preventative if the hands are grasping the opposite components.
- Holding hands behind you opens up the front and might convey confidence. Tension can also be seen in hidden hands. When one hand grips the other arm, the tighter the grip and the higher the hold define how much stress exists.
- Both hands can express a variety of desires. For example, making a fist with one hand and holding it back with the other indicates restraint from punching someone or something else.
- Deceitful individuals frequently try to keep their hands in check. If they remain motionless, you may become suspicious, with one often clutching the other. Another signal could be keeping them at bay. These are merely possible indicators; keep an eye out for further clues as well.

Control

•	A hand with the palm facing downward might figuratively constrain or grasp the other person. It could be a command, such as "Stop this now!" It could also be a request, such as "Please wait." This is also seen in the leading hand on a top handshake. Palms down while slanted on a desk usually denotes dominance.

•	In a less nuanced manner than the palms-down symbol, an outward-facing hand toward people pushes them away or fends them off.

•	A pointing hand or finger indicates where a person should go.

Hiding

•	Individuals can conceal their hands by putting them in their pockets, behind their backs, beneath their legs, or on the table. Hands are commonly used in communication, and hiding them may indicate a desire not to collaborate or communicate. "I don't agree with you," they may say, or "I don't want to talk to you."

•	Individuals may conceal their hands as an intentional act of defiance, such as putting their hands in their pockets. Liars may keep their hands hidden for fear of exposing themselves.

•	Hiding one's hands may also be a form of listening, conveying the message, "I want to listen, not talk."

- Hands behind the back or in pockets can also indicate a state of ease and a desire not to speak.

Fingerprints

Fingers are very flexible and can detect small signals. Here are a few examples:

Pointer

A pointing finger denotes orientation. Long distances might be covered by pointing the finger upward in a diagonal motion, similar to launching an arrow. Prodding and pointing at others are both considered intimidating and impolite. Angry people tend to point more. This pointing involves pointing at oneself when they feel insulted or injured, as well as pointing at people they believe are guilty.

Prod

Prodding can act as a stiletto knife, piercing forward at the other person. The index finger is most commonly used;however, the middle finger is also employed. Prodding is typically menacing and misconstrued as a personal attack. The prod can also be used to indicate a missing object by pointing downward. It is not as frightening as pointing directly at a person.

Rudeness

The middle finger pointing up denotes a penis and implies a curse. The small finger in this gesture means that the other person has a tiny penis. It is occasionally used as a derogatory symbol from a lady to a male. The first two fingers pointing upward while the palm faces inward denotes f**k off. The palm towards the other person, on the other hand, denotes peace.

Thumbs-up

•	A thumbs-up indicates agreement and approval. A thumbs-down suggests a lack of understanding. When held sideways, it conveys a sense of ambiguity.

•	When crossing arms or holding a single hand over the chest, a thumbs-up is a discreet approval symbol. It can also be used to invite people to demonstrate their support for what you're saying.

•	When you put your hands in your pockets, your thumbs usually protrude, indicating that you are confident, in control, and calm. As a result, the gesture could be interpreted as a message of warmth and authority.

•	Giving a thumbs-up signifies sexual attraction in some cultures. It may be considered impolite in other cultures.

Other Indications

- Crossed fingers indicate optimism.
- Fingernail inspection conveys apathy and boredom.
- Fingers fluttering can represent uncertainty.
- Fidgeting fingers can indicate stress or boredom.
- Finger sucking is a reversion to breastfeeding and childhood. It may also convey sentiments of inadequacy and fear.

Handshakes and Hand Gestures: Basic Interpretations

The way a person shakes hands, like the way they write, reveals something about their inner essence. You may make effective use of this knowledge if you are aware of what each handshake indicates about the people with whom you are dealing. Here are some examples of handshakes and what they mean:

Dominance

Dominance is demonstrated by placing one hand above the other, holding the individual with the other hand, and extending the holding.

Affection

The time and speed of the shake, touching with the other hand, and vigorously smiling show affection. Affectionate and domineering handshakes are similar, which might lead to a perplexing situation in which a dominant individual appears excellent.

Submission

Submission is characterized by a floppy hand, palm up (which may be sweaty at times), and a quick withdrawal.

Handshake Varieties

Fish that have died This handshake contains no energy, squeeze, shake, or pinch. It gives the impression that you are clutching a dead fish rather than a hand. This handshake has been linked to low self-esteem.

Sweaty palms

When a person is anxious, their nervous system becomes overactive, resulting in sweaty palms.

The Two-Handed Clasp

Politicians commonly use this handshake. It's a handshake that conjures up images of words like "friendly," "trustworthy," "warmth," and "honesty." If your hand stays on your hand, the handshake is genuine. If the hand moves to your arms, wrists, or elbows, they want something from you.

Remove the brush

This handshake consists of a quick hold followed by a release that appears to be pushing your hand aside. The handshake suggests that your purpose is unimportant.

Controller

This type of individual is a controller if you feel him tugging your hand toward him or guiding it to another direction or a chair. It suggests that they must have command over both animate and inanimate objects in the room, including you.

Crusher of Bones

This type of handshake, which involves squeezing your hands until you cringe, is intended to scare you. You don't have to act weak in front of these people. If you demonstrate your strength, they may even respond positively.

Vice President's Finger

When someone clutches your fingers rather than your entire hand, the goal is to keep you away from them. These people are usually safe. If they crush your fingertips, it is a demonstration of personal power designed to keep you at bay.

The Right-Handed Shake

Instead of holding his hand vertically, this shaker has his hand horizontally, so it is above yours. This gesture suggests he believes he is superior to you.

Claw of Lobster

The other person's fingers and thumb make a lobster claw-like contact with your palm. This person is afraid of deep ties and may struggle to form relationships. Allow them time and allow them to open up when they are ready.

The Pusher's alias

While this person gives you a handshake, she spreads her arms, making it impossible for you to come close. This type of person needs their own space and is refusing to let you in. If you want to be friends with them, you must give them the emotional and physical space they require.

CHAPTER 4

LEGS

Here's a question for you: "Which region of the body do you believe will provide you with an accurate reading on a person's genuine intentions?" The majority of people will unambiguously point to the face. They are, however, incorrect. Our legs are the most truthful portion of our bodies, according to research. It is true that the greater the distance between a body component and the brain, the less conscious we are of what it is doing.

We are trained from a young age to constantly put on a brave front, smile, and suffer the agony. Perhaps we were instructed to smile and express gratitude when our grandmother gave us that hideous sweater for Christmas. Please accept my apologies, Grandma. It's no wonder that as we grew older, we became adept at concealing our facial expressions.

However, we never learned how to hide our feelings with our legs, which is why it is challenging to imitate our leg movements. For example, a person can appear calm and put on their best poker face as their foot continually taps the ground, showing their frustration at being unable to leave.

Why Are Our Legs Such Good Reflectors of Our Emotional State?

Everything comes down to evolution. Since the first mcn began walking upright, our legs have enabled us to run, kick, swivel, jump, and do a variety of other actions. Our legs have aided us with two essential tasks: running away from danger and moving ahead to seek food. In other words, our legs are designed to pursue what we desire and avoid what we don't.

The legs indicate a person's readiness to stay or exit a conversation. Leg motions are visible in youngsters due to their heightened emotional state. Let's look at one of the most straightforward situations of how our legs reveal our mental condition.

A poker event was broadcast on television a few years ago. I saw him deal a firm hand. His feet were hopping and squirming beneath the table, like a small child on vacation. He put on a stern "poker look" above the table. The other players, who couldn't see his frantic leg movements beneath the table, called his bet and lost their money to him.

When we observe people, we frequently fail to notice their feet. What we don't realize is that our leg movements reflect our emotions.

From an angry person's attitude to a child's bashful feet when greeting strangers to a father's nervous pacing in the delivery room, all of these signals disclose our emotional state and help us perceive it in others.

So, if you want to comprehend the environment around you, look at other people's feet. Let's look at the important nonverbal messages of the feet and legs.

Displays of Excited Feet

For example, in a poker event, one of the players was able to hide his facial expression but couldn't stop the wiggling and bouncing off his legs in enthusiasm. The eager foot display is the name given to this nonverbal action.

People exhibit this leg movement after hearing or seeing something that has a good impact on them. It is a clear indication that the person believes he is in a better position to achieve what he wants from the other person.

So, how do you identify an enthusiastic foot when it's not safe to glance under the table? Before I respond, it is critical to understand that not every animated foot display signifies excitement or happiness.

It might also be an indication of anxiousness or impatience. When a person learns good news, the intensity of their leg movements rises. This is an indication of happiness or enthusiasm.

Leg-Shift Indicator

We gravitate toward what we like and find pleasing and away from what we find disagreeable. You can use this information to determine whether or not others are pleased to see you.

Here's a simple test to try: walk toward two people who are having a conversation. Make sure that they are people you've met before. So approach them and say, "Hi." You're not sure if they want your business right now. How can you tell what their genuine feelings are about your company? Examining their feet and body language.

If they turn their torso and feet to face you, they embrace your company. They would want to be left alone if they merely twist their hips to say hello without pointing their feet toward you.

This is also vital during talks. When a person moves his feet away from you and toward the exit, it indicates disengagement or a wish to leave the conversation. When someone rolls their feet away from you, it could mean that they no longer want to be with you. Perhaps you said something irritating or offensive.

The Knee-Clasp Demonstration

This leg movement indicates someone is about to leave or conclude a conversation. It is a sitting position characterized by a forward torso lean followed by the placement of both hands on the knee in a knee clasp. When you notice this in someone, it means they are ready to wrap up the meeting and depart. Take heed of this cue, especially if it comes from a superior.

The Leg Display that defies gravity

We looked at the nonverbal indications that people give out when they don't want to be near you. How can we use nonverbal leg signals to determine when someone is happy to see us? I'm sure you think it's simple to spot it. So, here's a question for you: what if the guy doesn't want you to know how thrilled he is to see you or a prospect?

When some people are happy to see you, their facial characteristics may not necessarily be evident. Instead, they make gravity-defying leg movements that disclose their genuine intents. Rocking up and down on the balls of your feet is one of the gravity-defying features. Walking with a spring in your step is sometimes part of it.

They may point their toes upward while keeping their heel on the ground.

Here's an interesting fact: persons suffering from severe depression rarely express this nonverbal cue.

Displays of Territorial Legs

Before we go into the leg display gesture and other sorts of dominant leg displays, I think it's important to understand the significance of personal space. We need to know why we tend to claim more territory for ourselves the more confident or superior we believe we are.

This brings us to Edward Hall's research on the relevance of personal space in humans and animals. He noticed that the more personal space one requested, the more self-assured and assured one is of their status. As a result, CEOs and higher-ups can carve out more room for themselves.

The rest of us are pretty protective of our personal space and dislike it when someone stands too near to us. When someone enters your personal space, your brain produces negative limbic emotions. Remember this the next time someone stands too near to you or vice versa.

The Territorial Leg-Splay Display

Leg splay is one of the most prominent and easily identified dominant leg behaviours. When people feel threatened or wish to threaten others, they become territorial. This leg action entails extending your legs wide apart to demonstrate masculinity and dominance. It is unsurprising that law enforcement personnel frequently assume this position in the presence of criminals and other officers.

The leg-splaying action gives a strong message to the astute observer that there are problems to be solved or that trouble is on the way.

Displays of Defensive Leg

Display of Crossed Legs

We will look at the significance of the crossed-leg position and how it complements the crossed-arm stance in presenting a defensive front. Here's an example to help you understand this defensive position.

There was a conference with two opposing groups of people, group A and group B, who had opposing views on a topic. When a spokesperson from group A took the stage to discuss the issue, everyone in group B assumed the crossed-arm and crossed-leg poses, as if commanded by a puppet. Group B was unconsciously rejecting what the speaker from the other group was stating.

As a result, if you want to persuade someone who has this leg position, you must first get them to uncross their legs. You can accomplish this by inviting them to sit next to you or by giving them something to grasp, such as a pamphlet.

The Ankle Strap

Most people assume this position as they are in a dental chair, waiting for the dentist to complete the work. Most people take this stance at the outset of an interview as well. Why? Fear, guilt, and uncertainty all contribute to this leg activity. In general, the anklelock posture is achieved by crossing your legs at the ankle.

Males frequently have a clenched fist resting on their knees or their hands tightly holding the arms of a chair.

The feminine version differs somewhat. The knees are held together, and the arms are gently put on the legs side by side. Most of the time, this gesture indicates that the person is suppressing a negative emotion, such as dread or doubt. When interviewees are uneasy, they adopt this posture. You must relax them and break the ankle lock in order to break the "ice" and get them to open up.

Sometimes folks will take the ankle lock a step further and lock their ankles around the chair while tightly holding the armrest of a chair. This behaviour indicates that something is bothering the person. In this situation, seek for clusters that show the same emotion as the ankle lock. A person who locks his ankle around the chair, for example, is inclined to move his hands down his legs as a calming action.

A person's feet might be moved from the front of the chair to under the chair. This withdrawal signal indicates that stress levels are rising. Over the years, I've concluded that when a high-stress question is posed, people will frequently withdraw their feet beneath the chair. This is a clue to the observant investigator or interviewer that the question is causing discomfort in the respondent, and they can choose to pursue that line of inquiry further. As the subject changes, the person's feet will gradually withdraw from beneath the chair, reacting to the limbic brain's relief that the question has been changed.

When used correctly, these nonverbal indicators can help you get a better read on individuals in a variety of situations. When you combine your knowledge of nonverbals from the legs and feet with signals from other regions of the body, you can understand what individuals are feeling and thinking and predict their next course of action. As a result, let us focus on the nonverbal messages of the hands and feet.

CHAPTER 5

OTHER BODY LANGUAGE INDICATORS

Aside from the precise gestures and actions, you should also start establishing a baseline to assist you in assessing the cues the body is expressing as a whole. When you observe a person, there is always broad nonverbal communication being sent. You may note how active, edgy, calm, composed, or stoic the person in front of you appears. They may exude a sense of dynamic energy and appear very optimistic and happy, or they may appear bulky and uninteresting. In this chapter, we'll look at some of the more noticeable body motions and what they mean in order to help you read people more appropriately.

The Cradle

- Chest protrusion can be interpreted as sexual or aggressive body language. Men do it to appear more dominating, intending to repel other bold men and attract members of the opposite sex. Women frequently do it to draw attention to their breasts, making them appear larger to catch men's watch.
- When a person inhales deeply, the lungs expand, making them appear larger and more prominent. This is primarily a male body stance. This can be interpreted as a hint of impending conflict. When a man does this, he often arches his back and holds his head up in an exaggerated manner to emphasize the puffed-up chest.

The Armpit

- Shoulder embraces are often non-sexual and occur between adult men or between a mother and her child. It is interpreted as a nonverbal expression of affection in which the arms are placed around the shoulders of another.
- Shoulder shrugs or rises are typically used to convey hesitation or scepticism. Depending on the context, it can be seen as apathy, resignation, helplessness, or even ignorance. The individual will raise their shoulders toward the ears.

The Hip Joints

- The hip tilt is a feminine movement. A lady will slump to one side to emphasize her curves, shifting her hips to the side. It's a straightforward technique of calling attention to her genitals. You see it a lot in the fashion business, and possibly the more exaggerated version known as the catwalk is all supposed to bring the focus to the gleaming genital region.
- Hip embrace occurs when two individuals (usually lovers) walk side by side with their arms around each other's hips. Take it as a strong display of intimacy.

Torso:

- Torso shielding occurs when a person employs their arm or an object to shield their chest from a perceived threat. This might be as subtle as holding a drink across the body or fiddling with their tie or cufflink or as blatant as a complete arm cross. Read it as a statement indicating that the other person is sheltering themself from something, and they disagree.
- Torso splay is a dominant bodily posture in which the individual lies back in a comfortable position with the chest puffed out and open, almost daring an attack. It might be interpreted as a sign of extreme comfort and the person signalling to you that they are in control of the situation.

Using Body Posture to Express Yourself

Did you realize that your body posture allows you to express yourself regularly? Posture refers to how you hold your body while moving and at rest. There are two sorts of body posture that you should be aware of. Body posture can be dynamic or static. Let's take a closer look at each of them.

Posture in Motion

It refers to the alignment of the body during activity or movement. In general, this entails moving the entire body in a specific manner. When it comes to dynamic posture, we want to make sure we move softly, that the knees are slightly bent, that the senses and mind are engaged, and so on. Walking, running, jumping, dancing and other forms of movement are all examples of dynamic posture. Our bodies are incredibly adaptable, and they are constantly striving for the route of least resistance, which is why bad posture is so bad since it inevitably becomes the default position, resulting in diminished flexibility, performance, and a slew of unnecessary ailments.

Posture Is Static

Static posture refers to how your body aligns when you are stationary or standing. Spend the next week assessing your position. Maintain a mirror in each room where you regularly stand so that you can see yourself. Is the shape of your shoulders rounded, level, or elevated? How about your mind? Do your knees cross your second and third toes? You want to ensure that your body can support itself with the least energy while keeping perfect form.

The position of your spine is the key to healthy posture, whether dynamic or static. You should become more acquainted with three natural curves. These are the curves of the neck, mid-back, and lower back. Maintaining these curves, rather than expanding or decreasing them, is the goal of good posture. How are you able to do this? Always keep your head over your shoulders and the top of your shoulder over your hips. Given how much time we spend sitting behind a desk or typing on a computer in our modern world, you should perform some check-ins during the day to ensure you are maintaining excellent posture. If you frequently carry heavy bags or move heavy objects, you must also preserve reinforcing proper alignment because these actions often throw us off balance.

Nonverbal Posture in Two Varieties

When interpreting body language, whether your own or that of another person, the two essential signals you may receive are open and closed. Open implies that the individual is not defensive and is more inclined and open to interacting. Of course, the closed stance means the inverse. To some extent, a person's posture form can tell you how confident they are and how receptive they are going to be if you connect with them. Consider approaching two individuals, both sitting at a table, since you required instructions to the restroom. One sat with his arms crossed and bent over, while the other sat with an open chest, head level, shoulders relaxed, and a calm countenance. Whom would you approach first?

Every time you interact with someone, or when you are about to interact with someone, read the form they have. They will be communicating either in a closed or open stance.

Posture of Closure

Whether or not the body's trunk is left open and exposed. That usually suggests that the person is amiable and receptive to interacting.

Pose that is open

When the trunk of the body is concealed by crossing arms and legs or hunching forward, that usually indicates that the person is not particularly friendly, is unwilling to engage, and maybe anxious or even hostile.

Notice how much easy it is to approach and interact with people who maintain an open posture. Most "cool guys" hold themselves in a way that makes them appear "open," as if you need to be around them. Examine how many people around you, particularly those you like, are displaying this position. Even if you want to approach someone you're attracted to, it will be more soothing and give you more confidence if the person looks open rather than closed. Now that you're aware of this pay more attention to the nonverbal posture you project when dealing with others in a social context.

CHAPTER 6

TIPS FOR SPEED READERS

Speed reading is a practice that aims to increase reading speed while maintaining comprehension and retention of information. There are various distinct speed-reading strategies for both books and online materials, all of which seek to read more efficiently.

Check out this step-by-step guide to improve your speed-reading abilities!

Improve Your Eyesight to Make Bigger Jumps

Do you know how your eyes move when you're reading? It's a jumping motion. Your eyes focus on one place on the line before moving on to the next.

The greater this leap, the better your reading ability. Beginner readers, such as children, skip only one word at a time, taking longer to complete each line. As a result, the first stage in fast reading is to develop your eye movement to be more comprehensive.

Proceed with caution.

The second step is to manage that anxiousness, that sense of obligation to comprehend the entire text. We will pursue this more, but 80 per cent comprehension is a fantastic target.

After all, rereading can be time-consuming, which is precisely what we want to avoid.

Furthermore, even if specific extracts are more perplexing, you may fully comprehend the overall idea of a piece. Then, once you've finished the text, go back and reread only the sections where you're unsure. However, if you repeatedly stop and go back, you will never complete reading.

Another essential suggestion is not to stop reading to look up words in the dictionary. If you're very curious about the meaning of a word, jot it down so you can look it up later. However, do not leave the text to look up words in the dictionary because it will take you even longer to begin reading when you return.

In the meanwhile, try to understand the term through context — you may not understand the exact definition of the word, but you will understand the message the author was attempting to express.

Stop Using the Words

The third step is to break a destructive behaviour that many individuals have, such as pronouncing the words as they read, either audibly or mentally.

This practice inhibits the development of fast reading because it requires you to read word for word.

The speed slows, and, as impossible as it may appear, so does the ability for comprehension. You won't be able to concentrate on deciphering what you're reading since your brain will be preoccupied with pronunciation. As a result, you'll have to review the same section numerous times.

If you're used to pronouncing words as you read, breaking the habit can be a time-consuming and challenging task. An intriguing suggestion is to read with a pencil in your mouth. With enough practice, you will be able to overcome this "craze" and discover how it improves your reading time.

Utilize the Skimming Technique

"Skimming" is the fourth phase. Instrumental English is a well-known approach, but it may be applied to any language for rapid reading.

Skimming entails swiftly scanning work for basic information such as the index, title, author, date of publication, primary subject, subtopics developed, graphics, and images.

This strategy allows you to rapidly assess any material and decide whether to invest more time in extensive reading.

If you are researching a given topic, for example, skimming will assist you in determining whether a particular article or book has essential information on the matter. Furthermore, you will be able to find the excerpts that interest you more readily.

Use the Scanning Method

Another strategy employed in English Instrumental is the fifth stage, "scanning." It essentially entails scanning the text for keywords, which in this case are relevant terms connected to the information you wish to extract from that content.

Assume you're reading a twenty-page paper on People Management, but the topic you're interested in is productivity. In that case, you don't have to read all twenty pages – which will very definitely teach you about a variety of other concerns that aren't relevant to you right now.

Instead, simply search the article for phrases relating to productivity, such as "time," "organization," "concentration," and so on. When you come across one of these terms, simply read the text that contains it. As a result, you may rapidly access information that is relevant to you and "skip" the rest.

Keep Track of Your Progress

After you've implemented what you've learned in the first five steps, the evolution of your speed reading will be determined by practice. However, in order to evaluate if it is working, you must keep track of your progress.

So, the sixth step is to get a stopwatch and keep track of how many words you read per minute. Keep in mind that the average reader reads at a rate of 150 words per minute. Meanwhile, a skilled speed reader can read up to 800 words per minute.

However, don't only keep an eye on the speed. Consider the utility of reading, that is, how much of the text you can comprehend without having to return to it a second time. Your target should be an average of 80% usage.

Remember that there is no purpose in speeding up reading and, as a result, losing knowledge of what has been read because rereading is also a waste of time.

Improve Your Focusing Ability

Now that we've covered the best strategies for speed reading, let's look at a few tips to improve your overall reading experience and, as a result, help you absorb more information in less time.

The ability to focus when reading is essential for productivity and avoiding time waste. The more you "plunge" into the text, the more you will understand what the author wrote. So, what happens if you check your cell phone notifications every two paragraphs? The encounter will be interrupted and resumed repeatedly, reducing your capacity to absorb and requiring you to take more time to understand what is read.

You lose twice as much time this way — the extra time it takes to absorb what you read, as well as the precious minutes lost with distractions like smartphones, computers, social networks, and so on.

If you frequently suffer from it, the trick is to make production a habit. To accomplish this, keep all distractions at bay when reading. This includes not leaving your phone nearby, not keeping your computer close by, and, if feasible, turning off the internet or at the very least putting your gadgets on aeroplane mode.

This is the time for you to focus solely on the text! The more concentrated you can be when reading, the better your ability to practice speed reading will be.

Locate a Quiet Area to Do Your Reading

The location in which you choose to read has a significant impact on the speed and dynamism of the activity, which is closely related to the danger represented by distractions, as previously indicated.

Noise from transportation, employment, an establishment – such as a bar – and even music can interfere with your ability to concentrate, causing you to frequently "stop" reading. Also, if you are reading in a public place, you will be promptly interrupted if someone speaks to you, even if it is a brief conversation.

Aside from being quiet, it is also critical that the reading spot be comfy. When you are at ease with reading, it is much easier to immerse yourself in the material and dedicate your complete attention to it. Another advantage of having a specific reading room is that it will be easier to establish reading as an integral part of your routine.

When you are tired, do not insist.

You may have heard that spending the night studying for an exam that would be given the next day is not very productive. At that time, the desperation of a few extra hours of study is no longer as crucial as the rest, which will allow the student to focus and remember more during the exam.

When we are fatigued, regardless of whether the fatigue reaches our site or brain, our concentration capacity suffers significantly. You will have to read and reread the same passage numerous times, and each line will take much longer to read.

The worst aspect is that you can pick up the material the next day and realize you don't remember much of what you read the night before. This is because a weary brain reduces its ability to retain knowledge.

So, knowing when to stop is a crucial aspect of fast reading.

When You Have Time, Read

What reader does not enjoy sitting in their favourite recliner for hours on end reading a book or even a relevant and high-quality text? However, as you are well aware, this is not always (or even seldom!) practicable.

Is this to imply that you are confined to a routine? Certainly not! It turns out that you don't have to beat yourself up for not being able to devote several hours of your day to reading. Begin to appreciate every spare minute, even idle time spent in lines, waiting rooms, or on public transportation. And how about going to bed a bit earlier every night and reading before bed?

A block of fifteen or twenty minutes that you would otherwise spend doing nothing becomes time well spent when dedicated to reading. Even if you can't read much each day, this allows you to make considerably faster progress in your lessons. Another advantage is that it will help you develop the habit of reading daily - and who knows, it may even encourage you to devote a few hours of your day to the activity.

Do you already read at a fast pace? How fast are you, and how well do you read? Do not be concerned if you have not yet achieved the objectives outlined here. Reading is a habit you should cultivate since the advantages are enormous.

Keep in mind, though, that frequent reading has the propensity to improve your vocabulary. And as your language expands, you will be able to read and comprehend more extensive materials with greater ease.

Speed Reading Secrets You Should Be Aware Of

Acquire how to read faster by ensuring that all of the information you learn is retained in your mind after a few days.

Respond immediately! Do you read quickly or slowly? Have you ever attempted to compute your reading speed? Have you ever heard of dynamic reading?

If you haven't already, you should. If you enjoy reading or rely on it for schoolwork, this advanced reading mode could be pretty helpful!

Dynamic reading is a form of reading that allows you to read a lot in a short amount of time. You might believe that reading quickly is simple, but you can't memorize it that way. As a result, dynamic reading assures this while not hurting its ability to assimilate information. We've put up some helpful hints to help you start enhancing your reading speed.

Recognize that there are various sorts of reading speeds. There are specific reading differences that you may not be aware of, and you must be. As previously said, more agile and focused reading minimizes the amount of time required for learning. As a result, it improves productivity and assures that all knowledge taught is retained in your memory after a few days.

This is vital for students, contestants, and even law and medical professionals who must continually read. However, this is not limited to a specific set of people. Dynamic reading can assist someone who already has a reading habit in becoming a reader with an enormous repertory.

It is critical to understand that dynamic reading is comprised of two primary components. Content speed and retention are examples of these. In short, reading too slowly can stymie your reading or study progress. Reading too quickly and not understanding the content is also not a good idea.

As a result, it is critical to balance reading at a rapid pace that does not interfere with knowledge retention. Excellent advice for anyone who wants to begin a dynamic assignment!

- Begin slowly.
- Every 15 minutes, you can read for free!
- Take only a few minutes out of your day to read.
- Walkabout with a book in your hand and read in brief bursts of time.
- While waiting for dinner to finish cooking, I read for 20 minutes.
- Read while waiting for the bus or, if feasible, while driving.

Dynamic reading will become second nature to you with time   and   practice!

CHAPTER 7

HOW CAN I BECOME A BETTER READER

It is not only about what you can accomplish for yourself when you read other people. It is also about what you can do to help others. You'll learn how to put people at ease, recognize when they need something they can't or won't tell you about, and, maybe most crucially, how to comprehend them and their wants, goals, and desires. There is no better gift you can give another human being than to understand and appreciate who they are and to be willing to deliver what they seek.

Set Your Judgment Free

When it comes to reading people, many factors might muddy your judgment. Biases, intimidation, and sexual attraction are just a few of the factors that can lead you to ignore your instincts and misjudge someone. If you admire someone, you may think their harsh behaviours are admirable, yet their activities would appear vile if you did not respect them. Allow nothing to cloud your judgment.

Men are less prone to pass severe judgment on attractive young women. With the goal of gaining their favour, they allow gorgeous young ladies get away with impolite behaviour. When you are attracted to someone, you are more inclined to overlook red indicators about them. Try to ignore your sexual attraction. Recognize that there are many gorgeous people globally, so focusing on one person's attractiveness is unnecessary. You simply need to look at an attractive person with more objectivity. Try to separate their character from their appearance.

You may admire someone because of their status or employment. Understand, however, that someone's status does not make them perfect. Do not be intimidated or perplexed by someone's social standing. They most likely ascended to their current position by being harsh to others. Read their personality apart from their status or job.

Being in an emotional funk might also cloud your judgment. When you are emotionally weak, you may be more challenging in your assessment of others. You may also be more receptive to acts of kindness from others. Unfortunately, manipulators are pretty good at detecting when you are upset and offering pleasant action in order to gain your favour. Don't let your emotional condition make you prone to erroneous judgment.

Emotional traumas can make it difficult to trust others. This is especially true if you've recently gone through a divorce or a horrible breakup. As a result, you may incorrectly judge the gender you are attracted to. You might despise every one of that gender right away. Do not be too ready to dismiss folks you do not know. Use your scars as a guide to reading people who remind you of those who have wounded you in the past, but don't fall into the trap of believing that the entire gender is awful. Give people a chance. Try to analyze them for who they are rather than who your ex was.

Don't only rely on behaviour.

Many people make the mistake of attempting to read others just based on their actions. However, behaviour frequently provides a partial and incorrect picture. You must consider someone's biases, mood, and even the situation's backdrop. You cannot always know all of this information, so don't even try to read someone based solely on their actions.

Sometimes the behaviour is incorrect because it is a forgery. Many people are skilled at putting on a show. They appear regular and upright while concealing horrifying underlying defects. Consider the majority of serial killers. They frequently go to work, maintain gorgeous homes, and appear to be completely regular individuals. When they are ultimately apprehended with a basement full of hacked-up bodies and torture devices, the entire world is outraged. Sexual deviants who are discovered accessing child porn are frequently politicians and businessmen who have promising careers and appear normal on the outside. While these examples are extreme, many people are skilled at concealing their negative characteristics behind seemingly ordinary conduct. As a result, you cannot depend your judgments on the outer behaviour of others because this behaviour can be manufactured and misleading.

Make a baseline

Try to establish a baseline for someone's typical behaviour. Keep an eye out for strange mannerisms that a person frequently exhibits. The quirks and habits that you notice in someone regularly establish the person's baseline. It doesn't take long to establish a baseline if you've honed your ability to read people through practice. Typically, FBI profilers will collect this information within the first fifteen seconds of meeting a person.

You can identify when someone is misbehaving based on this baseline. When someone behaves unusually, you can tell that something is wrong. Perhaps the individual is deceiving you or is upset about something.

It is difficult to establish a baseline on someone if you have not had the opportunity to observe him over time and are not yet competent at reading individuals in a matter of seconds. As a result, it's a good idea to keep an eye out for unusual behaviour. Unusual behaviour may be a quirk, or it may be a symptom of something more sinister, such as dishonesty. You might wish to ask other people who know the person well if this is typical of him. If you can't do that, you'll have to rely on your instincts. However, don't make too many assumptions about people based on their conduct.

Simply asking someone how they are doing today can help you establish a baseline. Keep an eye on how the person reacts. You can then figure out what their typical demeanour is. The more you communicate, the more you'll learn about the person's starting point. Is his eye twitching frequently? Is he fond of making hand gestures? Is he typically eloquent, or does he stutter? In addition, pay attention to the speed with which he speaks in everyday conversation, as well as the tone and pitch of his voice.

To recognize when someone is acting inconsistently, you must first create a baseline. A baseline also tells you how a person behaves in typical situations. If a person is regularly nervous, you can decide whether or not you want to be around someone who is frequently worried and, as a result, insecure with social anxiety. If a person is habitually unpleasant and abrupt, you can decide if you want to deal with that type of conduct in the future.

Things can be deduced from the initial reaction.

Of course, strangers are more likely to be anxious in their initial interactions with you because they do not know you well. However, a person's initial reaction to you reveals a lot about how he thinks about himself and how he feels about other people. This initial reaction reveals any hang-ups he may have, as well as the guard he puts up to protect himself or the façade he puts up to attract those he meets for the first time. As a result, his reply reveals a great deal about who he is as a person and what you may expect from him as you get to know him more.

If he is first nasty, for example, he may soften and become kinder to you, but you know that at the bottom, he is wary of new people. You may then question why he is on guard. He is most likely a sensitive and insecure person with much emotional baggage — he feels compelled to appear rough and irresponsible in order to avoid being harmed.

People who are remarkably articulate and charismatic frequently have a lot to hide. They are excellent at being around others while concealing their true selves. They have created conduct that is meant to entice individuals. Charming behaviour is frequently a sign of manipulative and deceptive personalities.

An exceedingly nervous individual is prone to social anxiety and insecurities. This person will most likely become more at ease with you over time. However, you should be cautious about putting too much faith in him.

Insecure people, on the whole, are untrustworthy and will behave in inappropriate ways. Unsure people have trust issues and act out cruelly because they believe they are not good enough. You are not accountable for another else's insecurities, so do not let such a person burden you with his troubles and concerns.

A person who appears overly calm is most likely suffering from social anxiety. Nevertheless, he is skilled at expressing composure to conceal his nervousness. People who are "too cool" should be avoided. Keep an eye out for those who simply want to talk about themselves. People who are concerned with themselves and refuse even to ask you questions about themselves are usually quite selfish. This behaviour will not change over time.

Someone's unpleasant behaviour will not alter with time, even if you encounter them for the first time. People like these are toxic and will only serve to drag you down.

A person who shamelessly talks about others when he first meets you is most likely a chronic gossip. It is unusual for someone to begin chattering as soon as he meets you.

Positivity and eagerness are excellent indicators in a new acquaintance. However, if someone talks much big game and brags a lot, you can presume that this person is attempting to impress you or even make up for something that he feels he lacks. Mild cheerfulness and eagerness are excellent indicators, but overemphasis is not.

A stranger's self-assurance and confidence is a good indicator. A person who is willing to introduce himself, look you in the eyes, and speak to you is usually confident in himself. He has gained good social skills and maybe a more sensitive friend, lover, or job associate as a result. While you should be wary of those who seem overly smooth and charming, someone who appears average yet is confident is usually a nice person to know.

Pose Specific Questions

If you want to get to know someone, feel free to ask him personal questions. He will most likely volunteer a lot of the information you seek. You don't even have to ask him questions to learn a lot about who he is as a person, what he enjoys, and what he hopes to gain from his relationship with you. This is why you should be an attentive listener.

However, if he does not volunteer the information you seek, you should inquire. It is preferable to ask specific inquiries rather than being imprecise. You face the danger of misinterpretation if you are ambiguous. There is no use or time for games as an adult. You know you can't read people's minds, and no one else can either. So, ask whatever you want to know without fear of being judged.

You don't want to come across as grilling someone. Rapid-fire queries can turn people off. Inquiring too profoundly about someone's life, family, or personality is also off-putting. However, anytime there is a pause in the discourse, do not be hesitant to offer general, socially acceptable inquiries.

Examine how a person responds to your queries. Because you've previously created a good baseline, you'll be able to see irregularities in his responses. If his gestures, tone, intonation, or eye contact abruptly depart from his baseline, it is a sign that he is not telling the truth or that a question makes him uncomfortable for some reason. Depending on your purpose in communicating with him, you can shift the subject or push it further.

The Selection of Words Is Critical

The way a guy speaks reveals a lot about how he is feeling and thinking. Pay attention to terms that indicate his aims and general state of mind. The words he picks tell a lot about who he is as a person and how he is feeling at the time. If you are meeting someone for the first time, keep in mind that the first meeting reveals a lot about who a person is on the inside. How he chooses to approach you right away shows a lot about who he is in general.

Someone who employs harsh, violent language is either aggressive or is currently in an angry mood. You never want someone to exhibit your anger when you first meet; this signals that the person may have a problem with anger control.

Someone who utilizes ambiguous language may be passive-aggressive and attempt to avoid a complicated subject. This type of individual cannot be direct. Expect games and behaviours such as avoiding responsibility. If this individual wrongs you, he will almost certainly never admit it or apologies. If he has a problem with you, he will probably never tell you directly but will instead hint about it or tell everyone else but you how he feels.

Another concerning symptom is when someone continuously apologizes or appears to accept responsibility for events. This type of person is highly sinecure and holds him responsible for everything.

Someone who employs egotistical rhetoric, such as bragging about winning "another" honour, shows his self-satisfaction. Keep an eye out for persons who exaggerate their accomplishments. These individuals are typically narcissistic and arrogant, or they are overcompensating for feelings of inadequacy.

A person who uses harsh words is likely to be too judgmental or a perfectionist. Keep an eye out for someone who nitpicks everything. This is a characteristic that will not fade with time. If anything, it will worsen over time.

The majority of people utilize "I" phrases more than any other. This is not a bad indicator, but someone who uses more "we" phrases is a better team member who wants to work with you. Someone who utilizes more "you" phrases is more concerned with you. This might be a positive indicator that someone is interested in pleasing you and getting to know you, or it can be a concerning sign that someone is attempting to manipulate you. To tell the difference, look for additional work choices. When someone asks you about your interests or who you are, it is usually an indication that he wants to get to know you or figure out how to please you best.

This is an excellent sign on a date, a new buddy, or a person you are considering hiring for a service. However, if he appears to be fishing for pertinent information with overly personal questions, if he keeps trying to find ways to commiserate with you so that you will confide in him, or if he is using fancy language and flattery to make you feel ingratiated and charmed by him, this is a bad sign that he is attempting to get an emotional hook into you to manipulate you.

Vague language is a solid indicator if someone is being deceptive. A person who refuses to answer yes or no questions is most likely lying. Someone who uses perplexing language is most likely purposefully generating a haze of ambiguity in order to conceal something.

CHAPTER 8

READING PEOPLE BY LOOKING AT THEIR PHOTOGRAPHS

There is no way to avoid people's photographs in the age of a constantly buzzing social media feed. People are going to take images of themselves, whether they want it or not. However, from the standpoint of a personal analyst, the good news is that you can get lots of hints for speed-reading people even before you meet them simply by learning to read their images.

Consider gathering information about the prospective employee before they come in for a face-to-face interview or learning more about a client before negotiating a binding agreement with them. How about choosing the appropriate date by learning about their personality through social media images? Every image of a person has a wealth of information, meaning, and an indication of their emotional condition. All we have to do is be alert enough to spot these hints. We can become so engrossed in the aesthetics of a picture or photography that we lose sight of the emotions underlying it.

This chapter tries to provide some insight into how images of people might be used to evaluate their values, personality, and behavioural features. There are some obvious and some subtle clues to deciphering a person's character from their images. Instead of perceiving the photographs as random shots, you will learn to locate more meaning and context within them.

Do Not Hasten

Because photography capture moments when time stops, you must carefully examine the image to avoid biases or false readings about something that may have happened in a microsecond. This may be in contrast to our fast-paced, short-attention-span, limited energy, and multi-tasking disposition. Before you begin evaluating people through their visuals, press the pause button in your head, take several deep breaths, and put yourself in slow motion. You must approach the art of people analysis with both curiosity and compassion.

Don't leave anything out. Examine the complete image. What draws your attention to the image when you first see it? What are the image's most noticeable features? Move your focus and awareness to the other areas of the photos gradually. Examine it from various angles and views.

Bring the image closer to your eyes to pick up on details that may otherwise go unseen. There are several small features that your vision may overlook if you do not examine them closely. Turning the image upside down or sideways allows you to see it from a unique angle, which can alter your entire perception of the image. You will notice things you would not have noticed otherwise.

Personal Reactions

What is it about an image that hits you the most the first time you view it? When you look at the picture instinctively, what emotions, feelings, thoughts, and sensations come to mind? As a caption or title for the photograph, consider a single descriptive word or phrase that reflects your instinctive reaction to the visual.

Do you believe the image depicts pride, fury, worry, relief, frustration, imprisonment, tiredness, success, elation, exhilaration, smoothness, rage, grief, or other powerful emotions? Your gut reaction reveals what you are thinking about the person.

One of the most significant elements while viewing or assessing people through their images is your instant or immediate reaction. You will, however, need to go beyond the first impression. To examine the person, you will need to use some free association. You are concentrating on all aspects of the image by using free association. Here are some questions you might ask yourself to help you assess individuals through photographs more freely.

What does the image make you think of?

What is the main feeling conveyed by the person in the image?

What memories, occurrences, and experiences can you recall from your state of consciousness when you look at the image? What would you call the shot?

However, when studying people through their images, keep in mind the terminology of projection used by psychologists. Projection is an unconscious process in which our sentiments, emotions, experiences, and memories affect our perspective of others. You may wind up projecting your feelings and experiences onto someone rather than attempting to discern their characteristics. This is especially true for more confusing visuals. You're not sure if you're empathizing with folks appropriately or just recalling your own experiences.

Our subjective feelings can sometimes get in the way of effectively reading individuals. However, overcoming this difficult position and recognizing when your own experiences and biases are interfering with people analysis will help you become a more prosperous people analyst.

Expressions on the Face

When it comes to picking up on other people's facial expressions, humans are intrinsically expressive. What is your initial reaction when you see the person's face in the photograph? Surprise, contempt, fear, sadness, anger, disgust, and happiness are the seven primary emotions acknowledged by psychologists. When studying people's expressions in photographs, keep these seven primary emotions in mind. At times, the indications are understated or delicate, making it difficult to pinpoint the immediate feeling.

Look for photos where the subject is unaware that they are being photographed, as this can be a more realistic reflection of their subconscious thought.

Relationships

Again, looking at images of people can reveal a lot about their relationships. There may be attraction or affection between two persons if one is leaning in the direction of the other. Similarly, if two people depend in opposite directions, the relationship may be cold. If you find someone clutching their lover's arm in practically every shot, they are probably afraid of losing their partner. It could reflect a strong sense of uneasiness or apprehension about losing their companion.

Attempt to predict a person's relationship based on their body language in images. This can be done in any public setting where you have time to observe people's body language, relationship equations, and emotions. What are their ideas, feelings, and attitudes toward one another? Is there a pattern in the way people touch, lean close, or look at one another? Is their body language indicating a lack of connection?

When it comes to people analysis, one of my favourite pastimes is looking at photographs of celebrity couples and attempting to read the nature of their relationships or personalities through their body language and expressions. I try to determine whether the image conveys intimacy, affection, and positivity. Or does it show tension, disharmony, and conflict? Alert, a well-known psychologist, feels that a picture can likewise forecast the destiny of a relationship.

Smiling, holding hands, and turning heads in the direction of their companion are all indicators of comfort. Hip to hip stance could imply that things are going swimmingly between the couple. How does the palmer touch work? If the lovers are touching with their entire hand, it indicates that they are close and affectionate. Touching your fingertips or fists, on the other hand, can show that you are distant and reserved. Crossed legs could indicate that they weren't feeling exceptionally comfortable or open at the time the photo was shot. A person who crosses their arms or legs in practically every photograph is likely to be distrustful, sceptical, cynical, and unenthusiastic by nature.

Personality Traits and Profile Photos

According to a large number of studies, humans tend to judge one other's personalities just at a fast glance. This is why first impressions are so powerful. It just takes three to four seconds for us to create an opinion about someone based on their verbal and nonverbal cues. Sometimes they don't even say anything, and we can pick up on personality traits subconsciously.

According to a recent study, you don't even have to meet someone once to create an opinion about them. All you need to do is look at their Facebook or Tinder profile photo to get a sense of their personality. Here are the top five personality traits revealed by a person's profile photo

The big five are about equivalent to Briggs-Myers in terms of scientific personality classification as Briggs-Myers is in terms of recruitment. This personality method divides people into five groups based on five essential characteristics: introversion-extroversion, agreeableness, openness to new experiences, conscientiousness, and neuroticism.

A quick peek at your social media profile photo is all you need to judge people on the five key dimensions accurately. PsyBlog's research found that there were highly clear and persistent patterns when it came to each of the five personality qualities, based on a scientific analysis of the profile photographs of thousands of social media participant personalities.

People who scored high on conscientiousness, for example, used photographs that were natural, filter-free, bright, and colourful. They were not hesitant to depict a wide range of emotions in their pictures. They conveyed more emotions through their photographs than any other personality type.

People who score high on openness will also take the most spectacular photographs. They are resourceful, innovative, and creative. Because of their ingenuity, they will spend much time experimenting with programs and filters. Their pictures will be more artistic, one-of-a-kind, and will contain more contrasts. People who score high on openness tend to have their faces take up more area in photographs than any other trait.

Extraverted people will always have broad smiles on their faces. They will use collages and may use vibrant images to surround their profile picture. Simple visuals with little colour or brightness, on the other hand, are a significant indicator of neuroticism. According to the blog, these images are likely to show a blank look or, in difficult situations, may entirely obscure their face. Among all personality types, agreeable people may appear to be the easiest to get along with. However, it turns out that they aren't excellent photographers.

Agreeable people are likely to publish unpleasant photos of themselves! Even if they have unfavourable photographs of themselves, they will be viewed smiling or smiling with a cheerful face. The visuals will be bright, upbeat, and dynamic.

CONCLUSION

Reading people is a crucial ability for everybody to have. This is because it will allow you to comprehend the entire message that someone is conveying to you during a conversation. This will put you ahead of the game in your interactions with others and help you establish yourself as a force to be reckoned with. Humans speak more nonverbally than orally, which is why, in order to understand what someone is saying genuinely, you must be able to read and interpret their nonverbal communication.

Listening to nonverbal communication is a skill that takes practice to master. As you are now aware, this mode of communication implies and alludes to far more than you are likely to hear or receive from an oral or written exchange with someone. Body movement, for example, can be used to convey a message in four different ways.

Mastering the art of nonverbal communication necessitates mastery of five concepts. These principles will not only help you discover nonverbal clues but will also assist you in accurately interpreting them. Without knowledge of these principles, you will be prone to making errors when it comes to reading others.

Being a skilled nonverbal communicator necessitates ongoing self-improvement. For example, emotional awareness, attentiveness, and consistent practice are all areas that you should work on and enhance if you want to become proficient at interpreting what people are expressing nonverbally.

Nonverbal communication has numerous advantages, some of which are as follows:

•	In order to supplement what is being expressed verbally,
•	To persuade others to believe something other than what you think,
•	To control what you're saying verbally,
•	To express your sentiments and emotions about a specific topic or a specific person, and so on.

Understanding personality types is another crucial step in strengthening your nonverbal communication skills. This will assist you in recognizing the motivations behind people's actions, allowing you to comprehend what they are saying.

While being able to read people is a valuable skill, combining it with charisma is much more so. This will allow you to connect with others, empathize with them, and establish a strong rapport with them. All of these are necessary, especially if you are passionate about assisting others in becoming the most refined versions of themselves.

Speed reading people is highly crucial if you are a leader, a politician, or have a career that requires you to interact with others. As a result, you must master and practice the necessary skills to become a good reader of people and nonverbal communication. This will put you in an excellent position to deal with people and bargain with them.